Kauai Travel Guide

*Experience the Best Places
to Eat, Drink, Stay,
Explore, and Discover
in Kauai, Hawaii*

by Kenneth McAllister

Table of Contents

Introduction

Right out the gate, let's clear up the pronunciation: It's pronounced as either ka-WAI or ka-WAH-ee, which is why it can be spelled as either "Kauai," or "Kaua'i," with the apostrophe signifying a third syllable.

According to local legend, the Hawaiian Islands were discovered by Kawai'iloa, a Polynesian navigator who came from... well, Polynesia. He had three sons: Kaua'i, O'ahu, and Maui. Kaua'i was his favorite.

The name, itself, means "place around the neck." This is in reference to how a father carries a beloved child, and how that child's arms wrap around his father's neck... or something like that.

From a geological standpoint, Kawai is the oldest of Hawaii's main islands, which probably explains why they had a head start in making it right. There's a reason they call this the "Garden Isle" and the "Island of Discovery." It's just that beautiful!

Like all the other islands, Kauai was formed by volcanoes. This one was formed some six million years ago, giving it time to sculpt its mountainous terrain. The highest of these is Kawaikini, which stands some 5,243 feet; while the second highest is Wai'ale'ale, located near the island's center.

The latter peak has the dubious honor of being one of the wettest places on earth due to the amount of rainfall it receives every year. Over the millennium, the rain has carved out a spectacular landscape of steep canyons and waterfalls. The most spectacular of these is the Waimea Canyon State Park — also called the "Grand Canyon of the Pacific." It looks like the Grand Canyon, too; albeit a far greener and wetter version of it.

Despite its spectacular scenery, Kauai is not the most populated of Hawaii's islands, with about 69,512 people as of 2013's census figures. Some suggest that there are actually more wild chickens than people, a breed brought over by the earliest Polynesian settlers which have thrived because they have few natural predators.

This does not mean that there's nothing to do on the island besides eating chicken, though. Far from it. Tourism is the island's main industry, followed by government and retail. This travel guide book will therefore fill you in on the best places to stay in, to eat and drink at, as well as to go exploring.

Bear in mind, however, that Kauai (like the rest of the Hawaiian Islands), is not cheap, even by the standards of the US mainland. This is due to the fact that most of what the state consumes is not locally produced. Technology, transportation, and even a lot of its food are imported, which impacts the overall cost of everything. That aside, there are many options available, depending on your budget. Let's get reading, so you can get travelling!

Chapter 1: Best Times to Visit

Since Kauai is not as (some would say "overly") developed as O'ahu, Maui, and the Island of Hawaii, there are generally fewer accommodation options available. Further, many of the spots (both the tourist meccas, as well as the more exotic and isolated locations) are not as easily accessible by road.

What this means is that it's generally one of the more expensive places to explore and to stay in. Whenever you choose to come, be prepared to rent a car, join a tour, take a boat, or even hire a helicopter to get to some places.

As with everywhere else, however, Kauai has its peak and off-peak seasons. During the latter, visitors are fewer which means that prices can plummet. If you time your visit correctly, your pocket doesn't have to hurt as much.

Bear in mind that because the island's topography is mountainous and varied, average temperatures depend on wherever you are. Besides elevation, average temperatures and climate also differs between the north eastern shore (which is windier, and therefore cooler and moist) and the south western shore (which is less windy and therefore hotter and drier).

THE BEST TIME TO VISIT KAUAI IS DURING:

1) Spring — April to June

Avoid the island in the last week of April. This is Golden Week in Japan because they celebrate three long consecutive holidays. As such, the island is teeming with them, causing prices to soar.

Aside from Golden Week, however, this is one of the best times to visit Kauai. The weather is generally cooler, but best of all, so is the cost of airfare and accommodation. A number of tours are also discounted.

2) Fall — September to November

Even this late in the year, Kauai enjoys average temperatures in the low 70s and 80s, making it another great time to visit. Since most would-be tourists stay at home during this period, it's not as crowded. Even better, average room rates at hotels can fall well below the normal $150/night mark.

DO NOT VISIT KAUAI DURING:

1) Winter — December to March

This is when most people visit the island, but it is also the worst time to do so. It's the coldest time of the year, and it rains a lot around December. Still, since they're willing to come, hotel prices can peak above the $500/night range.

2) Summer — July to August

The temperatures are blistering, but the tourists love it. This is also family season, with prices and tours to match. Unless you enjoy the planes, buses, hotels, and beaches with screaming children all over the place, save your money and wait for them to get back to school.

3) National Holidays

Hawaii celebrates both federal and state holidays, and while these are generally brief, inter-island travel spikes at this time. While this is good for Kauai's economy, this is not so good for you unless you have deep pockets, of course.

Besides the usual list of holidays observed on the US mainland, such as Independence Day (July 4) and Labor Day (fourth Thursday of November), there are three local ones that greatly impact the cost of transportation and accommodations throughout the islands. These are:

a) Prince Kuhio Day (March 26)
b) King Kamehameha Day (June 11)
c) Admission Day (third Friday of August)

A few more holidays have been imported by the immigrant community, but they are not recognized as state-wide holidays. Nevertheless, they can impact prices throughout the islands. These are:

a) Chinese New Year (January to February, depends on the lunar calendar)
b) Girl's Day (March 3)
c) Buddha's Birthday (April 8)
d) Father Damien's Day (April 15)
e) Boy's Day (May 5)
f) Samoan Flag Day (July 11)
g) Obon Festival (July through August)
h) Pearl Harbor Day (December 7)

Chapter 2: Accommodations on a Budget

Unfortunately, Kauai's version of "cheap" is not the same as what those on the American mainland are used to. Nature and underdevelopment, the island's main attractions, are the very things that keep prices high. Fewer hotels mean less competition, so average costs tend to be steep. The average cost of accommodation is usually just below $200/night. Again, however, it depends on the season.

Before you despair, there are indeed cheaper options available. As a general rule of thumb, avoid the south side (the Po'ipu area) which is also called the "Sunny South Side." The same goes for the north shore in Princeville and Hanalei. These are the more developed parts of the island, so this is also where you'll find the more upscale resorts and hotels.

If you're travelling with family or with a group, you can save money by renting a house, an apartment, or a room in either. These usually come with a functional kitchen, though no room service is provided, of course. A good place to get started is with TripAdvisor's vacation rentals page. HomeAway also has a section on Kauai that you might also want to check out, as does VRBO.

For those of you who absolutely need a hotel and all of its amenities but don't have deep pockets, Oyster and TripAdvisor have some great options available. Just remember that prices vary depending on the season.

If you're travelling alone, there are several budget options that are generally (heavy emphasis on "generally") well recommended. In Kapa'a, there's the Aloha Orchid Bed 'n Bath ($55/night), the Hibiscus Hollow ($50/night), and the Honu'ea International Hostel ($20 for a dorm and $50 for private rooms). Lihu'e has the Motel Lani (allegedly the island's first hotel at $55 to $70 a night) and the Tip Top Motel & Bakery ($45/night).

For those who prefer getting off the beaten path, the Koke'e State Park boasts Camp Slogett at $10 to $65 a night. The camp is actually a YWCA, but don't let the "W" scare you off if you're a man. All YWCA accommodations are open to both sexes, though they are often kept in separate rooms if they're not married.

A final option is to pack your camping gear and stay at any of the many camping sites throughout the island. You have to get permission, however, and abide by their various rules, though prices range anywhere from $5/night to $25/night. Check out the

state government's website if you want to explore this option:
www.kauai.gov/government/departments/parksrecreation/campinginformation

Chapter 3: Tips to Save on Food and Drink

Although the island is a tropical paradise which grows food all year long, much of what it produces is exported. Fortunately, there's still a bit left around for locals to buy, but again most food (like virtually everything else) is imported.

If you're coming from the US mainland, expect everything in Hawaii to cost an average of 30% more. This is due to:

(1) shipping fees, (2) which in turn forces retailers to maintain bigger inventories, (3) which takes up more space on a state with some of the most expensive real estate values due to limited land, (4) the higher cost of electricity (44¢ per kilowatt hour compared to the national average of 12¢ in 2012), and (5) the state's 4% excise tax.

This means that if you're planning to go to Kauai to enjoy the iconic Hawaiian luau, it'll cost you dearly. Most Hawaiians don't have luaus on a daily basis, anyway. Such is reserved for special occasions, as well as for wealthy tourists. As such, most who visit the islands know that food can really cut into their vacation budget. Fortunately, there are ways around this.

Locals make do by shopping at farmers' markets, roadside stands, big brands like Costco, Sam's Club, and Big Save, as well as drinking tap water instead of buying bottled water. Tap water throughout Hawaii is generally safe and with all the mineral springs they have throughout, is quite healthy (but ask the locals, first).

Packing your own lunch, especially on long excursions, is another recommended trick. There are, however, many tiny and therefore affordable mom-and-pop food stalls that dot the island.

Chapter 4: Some Affordable Dining Options

If cooking and eating cup noodles for the duration of your stay is not your thing, there are some (comparatively) cheaper options available that many locals and budget tourists swear by. The following establishments are still open as of October 2014, and are loved because they can get you full for under $20 per person.

1) Tahiti Nui Hanalei Restaurant & Bar

Opened in 1963 and maintained by the same family, Tahiti Nui has become a local institution. This is a fusion restaurant, specializing in Hawaiian, Thai, and Italian dishes. Located right beside the Hanalei Pier on Kuhio Highway, they pride themselves on their fresh seafood, casual atmosphere with outdoor dining, and rather outdated but charming Tiki bar decor.

2) Kilauea Fish Market

Located at the end of Kilauea Road, this very modest-looking, one-story, scrupulously clean shack with outdoor seating serves fantastic, fresh seafood. While different people rave over various dishes, this place's specialties are their homemade teriyaki sauce and sesame island dressing — which many swear are addictive.

3) Kilauea Bakery & Pau Hana Pizza

Located in the inner plaza of a small shopping center, it actually looks like a house with indoor and outdoor dining, complete with a balcony where you can sit on stools. Plenty of weird signs and memorabilia like a lower-end smaller version of TGIF. They also have some gluten-free items available, and if an entire pizza is too much for you, you can buy it by the slice. A typical lunch special with a drink and desert will cost about $10 per person.

4) Duane's Ono-Char Burger

It's actually a hole in the wall: a one-story structure painted red and white. This is a typical roadside mom-and-pop operation with outdoor dining (but no toilet) and the ubiquitous wild chickens in the yard. Opened for business in the 1970s, it has nevertheless become a favorite institution with the locals.

5) Monico's Taqueira

Despite the outdoor wooden benches, this one's definitely considerably more upscale. Monico

Hernandez is the proprietor and chef who grew up in East LA. While the specialty is Tex-Mex, there's a bit of an Asian twist to his dishes, such as fried spring rolls served with guacamole dip. Though food prices are reasonable, the items served at the bar require deeper pockets.

6) Hukilau Lanai

Located in the Kauai Coast Resort in Kapaa with its own poolside, this is definitely more upscale. Fortunately, their appetizers and some of their specials fall beneath the $20 range. Wine lovers can enjoy their wide selection at under $20 a bottle, but if it's just by-the-glass you're after with your meal, then prices vary from $5.75 to $6.

7) Kaua'i Community College

If you'd like to get a taste of fine dining without going broke, head on over to the college during the school season. Their Culinary Arts Program serves lunch daily from 10 am to 1 pm, but they also have a fine dining option if you want something more upscale.

An average three-course menu based on Cordon Bleu standards gets you an appetizer, an entree, and a dessert for $17.50. Since the food is cooked and served by students, you are asked to complete a comment card after your meal. For this option, however, you have to call ahead and make a reservation.

8) Hamura's Saimin Stand

This one is special. Opened for business in 1951, Hamura's has remained stuck in that era, and is yet another institution. A no-frills (and not very clean) establishment, it is the place where locals rub shoulders with politicians and celebrities, because of the food. Fortunately, such august customers have not affected their prices.

Saimin is the Hawaiian version of noodle soup and is the state's official dish. During the 1950s, America imported many Asians to work on Hawaii's booming plantations, and many stayed. Today, this dish carries with it the history and nostalgia of those settlers.

It's made of soft wheat egg noodles served with hot sauce, green onions, Spam, some local ingredients, as well as others from Asia. The dish is hard to place because it is a blend of virtually every culture that makes up the islands today. It is basically a combination of Filipino pansit, Chinese mein, and Japanese ramen, making it quintessentially Hawaiian.

Since Hamura's contributed to the development of this dish, it is an official historic place of interest. In 2006, it received the James Beard Foundation's (a culinary organization) award as one of America's Classics.

9) Lihue Barbecue Inn

A bit on the higher end, this is another institution, and despite its name, does not serve barbecues, for some reason. It's been around for 74 years (as of 2014), and serves rather generous portions. Their specialty is Japanese and Hawaiian food, as well as salads and excellent pastries.

10) Mark's Place

Not normally on the tourist circuit, this hard-to-find place is located in an industrial park and caters mostly to construction workers and locals in the know. Prices are low, but servings are generous. There's very little seating available inside, since the place is meant for take-out, but there are picnic tables with umbrellas outside if you'd rather eat onsite.

11) Keoki's Paradise

Despite the high-end decor and ambience (think of a Las Vegas rendition of the Hawaiian stereotype, complete with flaming torches), some of their dishes have surprisingly reasonable prices. They have a wide variety of items on their menu, but besides fresh seafood, they don't really have a regional specialty.

12) Sheraton Kauai Point

This hotel has three restaurants, each with its own bar, and one cafe: the **Link@Sheraton Café**. If you're on a budget, avoid **RumFire's**, which charges a premium for its spectacular 180° panoramic view of the beach. **Lava's on Poipu Beach** is more reasonable, though alcohol prices are rather steep.

If you want to splurge and experience a Hawaiian luau, complete with hula dancing, then head on over to **Auli'i Lu'au**. It's an all-you-can-eat buffet which costs $99.75 per person. That fee includes refills on drinks, including some alcoholic ones.

13) Sueoka's Store and Snack Shop

Another institution for the last 90 (plus) years, this is where the locals in Koloa go to for their stuff. If it's a meal you're after, a burger can set you back $1.95, while a plate lunch of meat or fish with rice or macaroni salad can cost about $6.50. There's no seating, either indoor or outdoor, but considering their prices and reputation for generous helpings of great food, who cares?

14) Koloa Fish Market

This tiny shop is right across the Koloa Post Office, and despite its complete lack of ambience (food is served in plastic containers), gets great reviews from even food snobs. As with Sueoka, there's no seating option available and the lines are quite long, since it's also a store. They actually make their own wasabi cream sauce which many swear by.

15) Gino's Brick Oven Pizza

Another fixture, this Italian eatery has been winning awards for its salads and pizzas. They have three branches throughout the island in Kalaheo, Kapaa, and Kapolei. Besides the usual Italian fare, each one also hosts a bar.

Chapter 5: Kauai's Best Beaches

This is perhaps the number one reason people come to Kauai, and the island certainly lives up to its expectations. That aside, again bear in mind that Kauai is renowned for its microclimates, so different beaches have their own pros and cons depending on their location and time of the year. If you're a surfing fanatic, check out the seasonal trends for the island's wave heights here:

www.kauaiexplorer.com/guides/seasonal_surf_trends

NORTH SHORE

It's best to avoid this area's beaches during winter when swells and currents are at their peak. While this is great for surfers who love that kind of stuff, most others should just stay clear.

1) Ainini Beach Park

If white sands are your thing, this area boasts miles of it. Even better, surfers hate it because it's protected by a reef which keeps the waves away, ensuring a safer and more relaxing swim. It is windy, however, making it a great place to go windsurfing. Since it's rather flat and shallow, you can actually wade all the way to the reef. As such, it's recommended for children and those new to snorkelling.

The beach itself has lots of trees which provide ample shade from the sun. Some facilities are also available, which include picnic tables, showers, and toilets, but no lifeguards. Because the waters here are not disturbed so much, underwater visibility is very clear.

2) Haena Beach Park and Tunnels Beach

A beautiful place for picnics and surfing, swimming is discouraged because there's no reef to tame the waves. If you really need to dive in, Tunnels Beach is just a stone's throw away. The water here is shallow, protected by a reef which makes it ideal for swimming and snorkelling.

3) Hanalei Bay Beach Park

You'll find this in Hanalei Town. Since it's a bay, the waves get pretty high here, making it a surfer's paradise. Currents are also strong, which is why they have lifeguards. Though a great scenic spot, they sometimes ban swimming when conditions become too dangerous. If snorkelling is your thing, this is not the place to do it due to the lack of a reef (no reef = few fish).

4) Ke'e Beach

You'll find this at the end of Highway 560. The presence of reefs make it great for snorkelling, but unlike Ainini, waves tend to be higher and currents tend to be stronger, hence the presence of lifeguards. Best to arrive in the morning since the crowds love this place and it can get very packed.

5) Lumahai Beach

Though one of the most photographed beaches on the island for its spectacular beauty, it's also among the most dangerous — renowned for many drownings. Summers are generally safer, but best check with the lifeguards before jumping in.

EAST SIDE

This is also called the Coconut Coast because of the coconut groves, once a staple of the island's early economy. This is also where most of the islanders live, making transportation easier and cheaper.

1) Lydgate Beach Park

Due to its location, this is one of the most popular beaches, and generally among the most crowded. To make it safer, they built a rock barrier out of boulders to minimize the waves. The result is two pools, a shallow one for children, and a deeper one for everyone else. You are not to swim outside these protected pools, and there are lifeguards about to make sure you don't.

2) Kalapaki Beach

If you like your amenities, then this is the place to be. Among the most developed beaches on the island, the oceanfront is crammed with restaurants, bars, shops, and hotels. The waves are generally shallow throughout most of the year, making it ideal for swimming.

3) Kealia Beach

Surfers should make their way to the northern end to avail of the great waves. If it's swimming you're after, the northern end also contains a ruined jetty which provides some protection from the stronger swells. Except for the paved walkway, picnic ground, showers, and toilets, there's not much else here, so be sure to bring your own food.

SOUTH SHORE

This is called the island's sunny side, which is where you'll find the resort area of Poipu. Besides beaches, this is also where you'll find the historic Old Koloa Town and get a chance to soak up some local history.

Poipu Beach Park

According to the *Travel Channel*, this qualifies as one of America's Best Beaches. It's also a tad expensive, since it's in the Poipu resort area, so you get the usual shopping, dining, and golf options.

It's also safe, as the waters are quite calm, making it ideal for snorkelling. December to May is humpback whale season, so you can either join a tour to get up close or watch them from the shore.

Do note, however, that there are endangered monk seals nearby. As such, some of the lifeguards do double duty as environmentalists, as concerned with the safety of the seals as they are with yours. You can easily spot them because they wear shirts emblazoned with the words "Monk Seal Watch."

WEST SIDE

This is where Captain Cook (the first European in Hawaii) landed in 1778. This area is separated from the North Shore by the Napali Coast, itself worth a visit. Since this is the drier part, the flora and fauna found here are different from the rest of the island. Many of the towns here are very small, but this place is also loaded with many historical sites.

1) Salt Pond Beach Park

This is a generally safe area for children because it's protected by reefs, but again it depends on the season. September is the hottest month, however, made worse by little in the way of shade. If you visit in the summer, be sure to bring your own beach umbrella. Facilities include toilets, shower, and a picnic area, as well as lifeguards.

2) Kekaha Beach Park

Due to the high waves, this is not the place to be for swimming or snorkelling, but if you're a surfer, then bingo! That said, the waves here are also famous for their ability to break surfboards, so consider yourself warned. If you still can't stay away, then take heart — there are lifeguards to watch out for you.

Chapter 6:   Must-See Discovery Spots

While its beaches are great, Kauai has other natural attractions worth visiting. Though most of these can be had for free, not all are easily accessible by car or by road. As such, some can only be accessed by guided tours, as well as with chartered helicopters. If you can afford the extra expense, however, they're well worth it.

Do note, however, that some areas can be closed due to weather conditions. As of October 2014, the Kula Forest Reserve remains off-limits due to damage from Hurricane Iselle.

WAIMEA CANYON

It was Mark Twain who called this the "Grand Canyon of the Pacific," and it's not hard to see why. The Waimea River, which begins at the Alaka'i Wilderness Area, cut out this spectacular landscape as it made its way to the ocean.

Located in the western part of the island, you can reach it from the town of Waimea by taking the Waimea Canyon Road (State Highway 550), or from the town of Kekaha by taking the Koke'e Road (State Highway 55). Once there, make your way to the three lookouts (Waimea Canyon Lookout, Pu'u Ka Pele Lookout, and Pu;u Hinahina Lookout) to see just how amazing this place is.

KOKE'E STATE PARK

Past Waimea Canyon, State Highway 550 goes on toward the Koke'e State Park with its over 4,000 acres of hiking trails along magnificent scenery. There are various viewing points along the way to make sure you get the full impact, but be sure to visit the Koke'e Museum, as well. Besides providing tours and explaining the history of the place, they also have a shop with some unique items.

NA PALI COAST

A state park, this one comes with many requirements, so you're often better off availing of a guided tour. No fee is required to get in, but to camp, you have to pay a fee. They sometimes close off portions due to weather conditions, but that aside, it is well worth a visit. For more information, visit their official website here:

www.hawaiistateparks.org/parks/kauai/napali

LIMAHULI GARDEN AND PRESERVE

This is for nature lovers who prefer less huffing and puffing. Since much of it is sculpted, it's generally easier on the legs. There's a fee ($40) to get in which includes a booklet so you can tour the place on your own. Besides botanical information, the book also explains many local myths and legends which makes for enjoyable reading.

Chapter 7: Historic Discovery Spots

It would be a shame to miss out on some of the island's local history. Although the arrival of Europeans changed local culture and admission into the United States nearly obliterated it, there's still a bit of the past left.

Ka Ulu O Laka Haiau

This is a temple devoted to Laka, the goddess of Hula. You'll find this on the north shore in Hanalei, near the Napali Coast trail. Much of the stone temple is in ruins, but they still hold hula dancing here. Bear in mind, however, that this is not for entertainment, but forms part of indigenous religious practices, so be respectful.

Waimea Town

This is where Captain James Cook first landed, and there's a statue of him in the town's center. If you want to know more about the region's history, visit the West Kauai Technology & Visitor Center, which also holds cultural programs and educational activities.

Old Koloa Town

Located in Poipu, this beautiful community was where Hawaii's sugar industry began in 1835. This paved the wave for the millions of immigrants (mostly from Asia) who have contributed to its local culture. Most of the buildings are wooden, colonial, plantation style structures that hark back to an earlier period. To find out more, visit the Koloa History Center.

Kauai Museum

Located in Lihue, the island's governing and commercial center, this is where Kauai tries to preserve its past. Spread out over two buildings, this place is packed with photographs and artefacts which chart the state's history from its pre-European past, its days of monarchy, absorption into the United States, and its plantation heyday.

They've recently added works by local artists, and provide guided tours. As of October 2014, they've begun installing air conditioning, so parts of the museum may be closed off.

Russian Fort Elizabeth

This is mostly just ruins now, but it marks an important part of Hawaii's history. The Russian

Empire made a brief alliance with the Kingdom of Hawaii in the 19th century, which the site details, complete with photographs.

Chapter 8: A Few Extra Pointers

Respect

As with all forms of travel, it is important to be flexible, to be respectful, and to keep an open mind. Remember that the indigenous culture is still alive and well. There are many places that look like natural scenic spots, but are actually sacred sites marked out with appropriate signage. Just as a Christian would be outraged to see church grounds desecrated, so locals would feel the same if you disrespect a holy site.

Safety

While the island is obscenely beautiful, the state's search-and-rescue teams report yearly increases in the number of operations they've had to mount. An overwhelming number of missing, injured, or stranded hikers are non-Hawaiian tourists who ignore trails or just have to dive into that alluring body of water. Download the state's free Hiking Safety in Hawaii brochure found here: www.hawaiistateparks.org/brochures before you set off on any hike or swim.

Marijuana and Nudism

The two common myths about Hawaii are that marijuana is legal and that nude bathing is acceptable, or that there are beaches available for nudists. While Kauai's climate is indeed ideal for weed growing, the state follows federal law, so being caught with the substance will get you in trouble. As to public nudity, it is also illegal.

Driving

Since the island is incredibly laid back, road courtesy is taken seriously and drivers allow others to enter traffic or to make left turns. The same courtesy will be expected of you. Honking is rarely done as it's considered extremely rude.

Directions

The cardinal points mean little on Kauai, so directions are based on the landscape, instead. *Makai* means "to the sea," while *mauka* means "to the mountain." It doesn't matter where you are on the island, or what road you're on, these two points of reference will always be used.

HAVE FUN!

Have a great trip – I hope you enjoy your time in Kauai! Whether you follow this guide or not, it'd be hard not to have a great time there.

Finally, I'd like to thank you for purchasing this book! If you enjoyed it or found it helpful, I'd greatly appreciate it if you'd take a moment to leave a review on Amazon. Thank you!

Made in United States
Orlando, FL
09 June 2022

18635955R00030